Rhetoric

Pat Grieco

Grieco

Other Books by Pat Grieco

The Art of Nauga Farming

Compulsion

Rhetoric

Print edition produced in the United States of America

Cover art: Pat Grieco

Print ISBN: 978-0-9997944-6-3

Pen and Lute
www.penandlute.com

The final approval for this literary material is granted by the author.

Library of Congress Control Number: 2018959204

Distributed Publication
Lexington, KY
Middletown, DE
San Bernardino. CA

Grieco

DEDICATION

For those who see beyond the words

.

Rhetoric

Pat Grieco

Grieco

Rhetoric

There are none so blind
as those who say they see
and understand
when they do not.
For there is certainty
in ignorance
and from certainty
does action come.
And it is in action
that our ends
become manifest.

Grieco

CONTENTS

A Short Step...1

It all begins… 3

Civil Discourse 5

The security of one 8

In the shadows 11

I kneel 13

Candidates...15

One...18

Dawn of the new age 21

With does color mean? 24

A Kind Man 26

Equality...29

Principled Realism...32

In servitude 35

God given duty 37

Rhetoric...39

Immigrants...43

Religious Liberty 45

Truth 48

Guns...53

A brave face...55

In for a penny...58

Heroes 61

When the caisson rolls 64

Rhetoric

We are all one 66

Accidental Extinction 69

Those who do not learn from history................71

Think three times 75

Blood and treasure 77

One Word..80

The coming season 83

The Heavens Wept...86

What value? 90

Imprisoned though my spirit be........................92

Your Right to Vote 94

Fever dream 96

A Short Step

It is a short step
from liberty to chains,
from freedom to oppression,
from cherished rights
to imagined wrongs.

Just one judgement,
just one democratic vote,
and all that was gained
may be lost in an instant,
rights trampled,
speech denied,
covenants broken
with no redress but law
no longer made or interpreted
for the common good.

Stability.
Security.
Safety.
All have been
the watchwords of tyrants
who have used them
to justify patriotic acts
restricting freedoms,
limiting access,
denying self-evident truths.

What is done to one
can be done to all
and we must be as mindful
of our neighbors' liberty
as we are of our own.

Rhetoric

Beware the knock on the door,
it may be for you.

Fear internment,
for it may yet occur
if your views are not in favor,
if your thoughts are not pure,
if you threaten the stability,
security,
the safety
of those set above you.

Rights change,
freedoms die,
and liberties vanish
with the well intentioned
stroke of a pen.

Be watchful.

Be aware.

Be careful,
for it is but a short step
from liberty to chains.

It all begins…

It all begins
with one person saying no,
with one person saying
not here,
not now,
not ever,
and the world changes,
not all at once
and seldom quickly
but it does
as no builds upon no
and refusal to accept
degradation,
humiliation,
subjugation,
is at last realized.

It does not come without pain.
It does not come without suffering
and the first to speak
is seldom praised
or even remembered
for their courage,
for their stubbornness,
for their willingness
to pay the price
for speaking out.

But without the first,
there are none who follow,
none to join a swelling chorus
of voices raised in anger,
voices raised in defiance,
voices raised in hope

Rhetoric

that what is wrong
will be righted,
that transgressions
will be redressed,
and a better world
will exist tomorrow
for all to share.

For there must be a first
before there can be a second
or a third
or the flood that follows.

It all begins
with one person saying no.

Civil Discourse

Let us not overestimate the value of civility.
Rather let us embrace rudeness,
the brashness of youth,
the excitement of adventure,
the constant renewal of change.

It is not enough, I fear, to be civil.
For it brings a pattern
to which we grow accustomed
as in a path long and well trod
by feet that know no other.

There may be new ground all around
but we will not move upon it,
will not acknowledge the possibilities,
the worthy nature of the endeavor
to be found if path were left,
perhaps not abandoned,
but neglected for just awhile.

Oh, civility has its place.
It is a mask
to hide the savage beast inside,
to train it,
contain it,
and keep a lease on longings,
to sequester desire and hate,
and fear,
and love
behind a wall of polite manners
and strictest order.

But the beast remains
and uses civil discourse

Rhetoric

as a means to hide its true intent,
its chosen course,
and hunts upon the proven path
whilst living elsewhere.

Civility shelters the weak
but it does not protect them.
But still,
the beast is restrained by civility.
It keeps to the paths it knows
and will venture upon no other,
even if its fate should be decided so.

Thus, innocent and beast alike,
prey and hunter both,
are lost if path should end
and unconstrained nature take its course.

Beyond the path,
beyond civility,
only brashness,
only adaptability,
only raw and brutal strength will prevail
as patterns shatter,
habits fail,
and new ground becomes old
with the trampling of it.

Strength and power hold different meanings
when one world ends
and need reshapes the new to its own ends.
We are seldom who we think we are,
with pretense and veneers
stripped away by necessity.

Civility hides us.
The untrammeled way

and existence
in the face of the wildness without
reveals us as we are.

In the end it matters not,
for we are either tamed or not
and well trod path or unknown wilds
make no difference to the fact inside.

We either hunt or not.
We are either prey or not.
We are either civilized or not
regardless of veneer or appearance.

For one must first survive to be civil.
One need not be civil to survive.
And those who confuse the two
seldom do so for long.

Rhetoric

The security of one

Why should you spend
your blood and money
to protect those less capable,
less well off,
less able to defend themselves?

Because if you do not
then no one
will spend theirs
to defend you
when it is your turn,
when the mob
cries for blood,
the wolf
is at the door,
or the bear
sees you as
just a light snack
before dinner.

The security of one
depends on the security of all.

They are inseparable.
To think otherwise
is both selfish
and self-defeating.

Selfish
because you place
your well being
above that of your neighbors.

Self-defeating

because, once your neighbors are gone,
they will come for you.

And where before
you could have stood
tall and proud
with those around you,
now
you can only cower
in the corner
attempting to hide
as the inevitable occurs.

The security of all
depends on the security of one,
each and every one
of those neighbors
thought less of,
thought to be too small
or weak
to be bothered with
or worthy of your notice
or defense.

Yes, you will spill your blood
and spend your coin
if the need should come,
the enemy be bold,
and the times be dire,
but it will be alongside them
as they spill their blood,
spend their coin,
fight to preserve
what is theirs,
and labor to safeguard
their families and friends
to secure

Rhetoric

a more welcoming tomorrow,
as tomorrow
they will stand with you
to help preserve yours.

The security of one
depends on the security of all.

In the shadows

They stood in the shadows
and whispered their concerns.
"Isn't it horrible…"
"How could they do such a thing…"
"Someone should say something,
do something to stop it…"
"That should never be acceptable
in this country…"

But when they stepped into the light,
they were silent.
They would not speak
of the concerns they whispered of
beyond the sight of folks
who looked to them for guidance,
who looked to them for truth,
who looked to them
for what was acceptable,
for what they should think,
and what they should believe.

They reconciled this silence,
this failure to speak of their concerns
with thoughts of their jobs,
with thoughts of their careers,
with thoughts that folks
really didn't want to hear the truth,
and that right no longer carried the day
in the face of those
who paid it no heed.

And when they prayed,
and they did more of that these days,
the beating of their martyred hearts

Rhetoric

reminded them of their humanity,
reminded them of their duty,
reminded them of the difference
they could have made
out there in the light
where all could see.

But in the shadows
where they whispered,
where they prayed
in the absence of action,
in the absence of resolve,
they sought comfort in the thought
that at least
it wasn't happening where they lived,
that at least
no one was coming for them,
or their families,
or their friends,
and they prayed
that they never would…

I kneel

I kneel because I respect the flag,
the anthem,
this nation,
and all it stands for.

I kneel because I believe
in equal rights,
in justice for all folk
regardless of color,
ethnicity,
or sexual orientation.

I kneel because of all those
who came before,
who gave their lives
to preserve freedom,
and guarantee liberty,
who dedicated their very selves
to give us this nation
that we celebrate
with every word
that is freely spoken,
with every act
that demonstrates
our fealty to its principles.

You need not agree with me.
You need not believe as I do.
You need not live
by the same principles
that I pay homage to today
amongst the crowd,
amongst the noise
and celebration.

Rhetoric

And that is the beauty of it.
That is the wonder of this nation,
that each of us,
regardless of who we are,
or where we're from,
or what we hold dear
can live together in harmony,
can live together as equals,
can share the common principles
and ideals this country stands for,
indeed, that it was founded on.

And so,
it is those principles,
it is those ideals,
it is that flag,
it is that anthem,
it is that country
that I support here today
as I silently,
peacefully,
kneel.

Candidates

There once were two candidates
eager to bring their vision of change
to the people.

Each brought a burning drive
to change the world,
to reshape it in a manner
more to their liking,
more to the way
they thought it should be.
Each trusted in their qualifications
to win the electoral fray.

One was well versed
in foreign policy.
One was not.

One had a long history
of public service.
One served only themself.

One had detailed plans for policies
on domestic and international matters.
One had vague notions
and changing promises.

One, for the most part,
told the truth.
One told lies
and created alternatives
to facts found bothersome.

One was demonized.
One demonized.

Rhetoric

One had endured
the fires of adversity
over a long career.
One lit those fires
whenever they went.

One offered rational choices.
One offered hope and fear.

One supported the ninety-nine percent
but spoke like the one.
One supported the one percent
but spoke like the ninety-nine.

One promoted diversity
and the rights of all
while seeking to protect
the poor and middle class.
One sought to disrupt
and sow confusion
while dividing one from another
by speaking to our lesser selves.

One wanted to protect the planet
and advocated for a green economy
and the new jobs yet to come.
One wanted to protect profits
and promised to return
to the industrial past
and jobs that had long vanished
with the changing world.

The choice was stark.
The choice was clear.
Truth versus lies.
Plans for the future

versus notions of a perfect past.

But in the end,
it didn't matter
if they were qualified or not,
truthful of not,
green or profiteer,
demon or demonizer.

In the end,
folks did not vote
for who the candidates were
but rather for what
they thought they were,
for what they wanted them to be.
They held their noses
and voted for the change
they hoped would come.

They voted for their pride.
They voted for their beliefs.
They voted for their fears.
They voted for their hopes.
They voted for their emotions.
They voted for their tribes.

And when it was all said and done,
they got what they voted for.

Rhetoric

One

We are either one nation
or we are many
and thus none at all.
We are either one people
or separate and divided.
We either speak with one voice
in one language
or we are but a multitude
distressed at being misunderstood
by those who do not share our speech.

We are a mixed folk
but neither black,
nor brown,
nor white,
nor yellow,
nor red,
or place of origin
or of birth
defines us individually
or as a group
with each person equal
and free within the mix
as laws bind together
and social contract
keeps us whole.

We can be religious
but cannot place religion first
for then we are but Hindus,
or Christians,
or Moslems,
or Jews,
or Buddhists,

and not truly citizens
for if faith
and the "laws of God" prevail
then the social contract is void,
freedom is lost,
and religious tyranny is assured.

We either hold allegiance to this nation
or we do not,
with religion and ethnic mix
holding no sway
on where our hearts must lay.

We are proud of where we came from,
proud of where we are now,
and proud of what we can be;
a secular state
that trusts in God
but is not ruled
by one vision of it;
a single, diverse people
with a common tongue,
a common heritage,
and a single future;
a nation that embraces all
and assimilates distinctive differences
into the greater whole,
changing while remaining the same;
a purpose and a reason;
a beacon and a hope;
a vision and a reality;
a contradiction and an affirmation
of many becoming one.

One allegiance
One people
One voice

Rhetoric

**We are either one nation
or we are not.**

Dawn of the new age

Democracy dies a slow and lingering death
with every lie believed,
with every scapegoat found,
with every district secured,
with every vote changed
or suppressed,
with every democratic norm
flaunted,
ignored,
or broken
brazenly in the open
or in the dark
of hidden conspiracy.

Institutions are no proof against this.
They cannot cry out when abused.
They cannot signal when perverted
or destroyed from within.
They cannot safeguard
rights or liberties
from those who would erase them,
who would use those institutions
to remove them,
one by one,
in the name of justice,
in the cause of morality,
or for the purpose
of imposing religious sensibilities
on the non-believing mass
that threaten civilization
with their liberal views,
their failure to conform,
and their humanity.

Rhetoric

Freedom is often earned in struggle,
soaked with the blood of tyrants,
drenched with the tears of the oppressed,
hard won by every martyr,
burnished by every victory
and every sacrifice that made it so.

But it often dies in silence,
freely abandoned
for the sake of power,
for a singular vision
of right and wrong,
for the lure of strength
in the face of perceived weakness.

When the end comes,
it is unexpected
in its suddenness,
in the ease with which it happens,
and the acceptance it receives.

Who needs freedom
if they are hungry?
Who needs liberty
if the hordes are at the door,
the enemy is within,
the lie is spoken,
and security achieved?

Democracy dies a slow and lingering death
but in the dawn of the new age
it disappears unnoticed
by those who could not keep it,
unwanted by those who end it,
unmourned by those
who placed no value on it.

In the end,
it becomes a myth.
It lingers in memory
as a legend,
a story for parents
to tell their children
but quietly
and in whispers
lest they be discovered
and denounced
as enemies of the new order.

In the cells of the dispossessed
will it be mourned
with tears of shame
and anguish
that it could come to this,
that hard earned liberties
should be forgot,
should be freely given up
by those who should know better,
that did know better
but did it anyway
with their silence,
by their vote,
by their acceptance
as norms were trampled,
institutions undermined,
and democracy died.

Rhetoric

With does color mean?

What does color mean to a blind man
when his only choice is darkness?

What matter day or night,
light or dark,
sun or moon,
if all remains the same
with eyes open or closed,
blind to the surrounding world?

How does one decide
the nature of the world,
likes,
loves,
hates,
when one cannot see it?

How does one tell
kindness or neglect,
quality or dross,
perfection or im
without the clues
that sight provides?

How does prejudice form
without the reinforcement
that vision brings?

How does one judge
a person's worth?

What matter looks
when soul is judged
by other, better things

and measured by a gauge
whose markings are felt,
not viewed,
unblemished
by perceived station,
state,
or place?

How does one sense
the pureness of the human heart
and trust
that all will be
as promised
when the noise stops,
speaking ceases,
and one is left alone
in darkness
once more?

What does color mean to a blind man?

Rhetoric

A Kind Man

He was a kind man,
broad of face,
with a ready smile
and a booming laugh
that eased the cares of those nearby.

He was a pillar of the community,
always there to help a neighbor in need
or to fix whatever needed fixing
at the town's orphanage.

He was an elder at the church
and devoted countless hours to prayer
in search of answers to the world's woes.

Yes, he was a kind man,
and so did not make her watch,
there among the trees
by the freshly dug hole,
as he killed her children
although there was no escaping their cries
and the thunder of the shots
that silenced them.

He had no choice.
It was his duty.
He had his orders.
If the woman and her children did not die,
it was inevitable
that he himself would be killed
and then his wife and children,
safely far from here,
would face an unkind fate
in a time devoid of sympathy.

He listened
as the echoes from his pistol
faded slowly
and the stillness of the day
returned to gently mock the scene.

He nodded at the woman,
sobbing now
on her knees in grief,
and watched
as she too was rendered mute
by single shot
from accompanying guard.

He nodded once again
and bodies were collected
only to disappear
into the waiting earth
where they were covered
with the piled dirt.

Done, he departed
leaving others to finish in his stead.

He drove in silence to the town
where he parked in his customary spot
and walked towards home
along the cobbled streets.

He paused
in the shadow of the old clock tower
to dig for change within his pockets
and gave all he found
to the beggar huddled there.

He would have done more

Rhetoric

but his wallet was in his coat
Still thrown across the kitchen chair,
forgotten in his need
to be about the business of the day.

His children squealed in glee
to see him move along the fence
that kept his yard separate from the street.
They grabbed and pulled at his clothes and legs
as he pushed the gate shut behind him
each eager for his attention
and the warm embrace of their father's love.

Soon satisfied,
they quickly resumed their play
leaving him to do the weekend tasks
allotted for this day.

Time passed.
He tended his yard with careful diligence
setting all to right
within this portion of the world.

Finished,
He sat upon his patio chair,
watched the children play
beneath the summer sun,
listened to the birds sing their silvered song,
and tried not to think.

He was after all
a kind man.

Grieco

Equality

When the water came
it didn't care
if we were white or brown,
red or yellow,
light or dark.

It didn't ask us
for our driver's licenses
or our passports.

It didn't matter
if we were citizens or not,
rich or poor,
young or old,
what faith we held,
or what our gender was.

The waters claimed us,
one by one
as they rose,
slowly at first
and then in a rush,
cutting off
all chance of escape,
severing all communications,
closing all routes out
as though they had never been,
leaving us alone
and desperate,
waiting,
in those final moments,
for help
that might not come.

29

Rhetoric

No,
the water did not care
about who
or what we were
before it came.
It simply swept across our lives
wiping them all away.

Help did come,
sometimes too late
but more often in time,
as folks fought
the fury of the storm
and sought to rescue
others from its wrath.

But still the waters came
until there was no room
to think of anything
but survival
and of those still trapped
somewhere in its midst.

The rescued,
in their thousands,
sheltered where they could,
cared for by the more fortunate,
sharing the generosity
of those moved by their plight
and the uniting force of tragedy.

But still the water waited
just beyond their havens
encroaching even there
until the thought of safety
narrowed to a dry place
to sit,

to rest,
to sleep
until order was restored
when the storm passed.

Eventually it did
but not before
the damage was done,
lives were changed,
and all that remained
were soggy remnants
of people's dreams.

The water will recede.
The debris will be cleared.
Homes will be repaired,
services restored,
and we will go back to being
what and who we were
before.

But for a moment,
as the wind howled,
the rain fell,
and the water surged
robbing us of all we had,
we were equal.

Rhetoric

Principled Realism

Do what you want in your own countries.
It is of no concern to us.
Kill who you want.
Arrest who you want.
Persecute, malign, or mistreat
who you want.
It is your business, not ours.

Your enemies are our enemies,
as long as you buy our weapons and goods.
as long as you invest money in our country.
as long as you do not send your unwanted
to our shores,
to our country
for us to deal with.

Keep your problems where they belong.
Solve them before they become ours.
Fight your own wars.
(We will arm you.)
Kill the bad folks where they live.
(We will help find them for you.)

Pay us
and we will be your friend.
Be our partner
or we will find another
who thinks more kindly of us
for the moment,
for this time when we need them
to fulfill our strategic and tactical goals.

Beware of principled realism
for it does not exist
in whole or in part.

As to principles,
we have none
or if we do,
they change as the need arises.
Our own self-interest governs all
and that will change,
as we do, over time.

As to realism,
it cannot be trusted.
For what is real
changes with our perception of it.
And our perception of your friendship
will be steady only as long
as you buy our goods and weapons,
fight your own wars
(while supporting us when we fight ours),
and give us a place for our ships,
our planes,
our tanks,
and our troops,
whenever we ask.

Beware.
For you may at some point
be on the opposite side of the equation
of self-interest,
of perception,
of weapons sales,
and friendship.

And then,
you will be enemy of our friend,

Rhetoric

the object of our shifting wrath,
and the focus of our
principled realism.

In servitude

One can be true to oneself,
or to a master,
but not both.

One can serve another
but to do so
one must subjugate their feelings,
their desires,
their needs,
to ensure the welfare
of what is served.

Compromise is the name of the game.
Compromise of principles,
compromise of hopes,
compromise of self
to serve the greater good
or ill
represented by the master.

All wish to be their own person,
to chart their own fate,
to be ruled by their own dictates
and not another's.

But in the end,
most must choose
to live well or un,
to eat or starve,
to protect their own
against the night chill
and the savage beast.

And so they choose

Rhetoric

and prosper or not
on the whims of fate,
the kindness of their master,
and the vagaries of the world without.

For it is a rare master
that will sacrifice their own good
for that of those who serve,
who toil in the shadows
so that the master may flourish
while they eke out a meager existence
or prosper based on the master served,
the task chosen,
and idle chance.

 And so, in the end,
when the mirror is faced,
the question is asked,
and the choice confronted,
will one be true to mirrored self
or choose a path less rocky,
less fraught with immediate peril
but no less certain in the dangers faced,
tasks shouldered,
and the loss of self.

Choose
and face a certain doom
or do not
and face one imposed by others
perhaps at a more
unfavorable time and place.
Both perhaps beyond control,
but each shaped by this one question,
this one choice,
this one decision,
"Who do I serve?"

God given duty

It was their God given duty
to change the world,
to remake it
in the image of their gods.
And so they proceeded
clothed in righteousness
and grace.

For they were the only ones
who heard the words,
knew what they meant,
understood what needed to be done
to reshape God's creation
and make it holy once more.

And so,
when the people
came to their churches,
to their temples,
and to their mosques
and asked for guidance,
they gave it.

They told them
how to pray,
what to think and believe,
how to live,
what to keep
and what to cast aside,
who to shun,
who to follow,
and who to kill
to make the world
a better place.

Rhetoric

And when the people
followed their direction,
in innocence and faith,
cleansing the world of evil,
they looked upon the reborn world
and found it
to be a mirror to their souls.

It was their God given duty
to change the world.
And so they proceeded
clothed in righteousness
and grace.

Rhetoric

In the swirl of actions
and reactions
and the tumult of the day
as crises loom
and danger threatens,
the loudest voices heard
are seldom the best
nor the most reasoned.

They may ignore our values,
the long path of history,
and even the Constitution itself.

They may seek to address
our lesser selves,
the parts motivated by fear,
incited by directed hatred,
and inspired by a resistance to change
and of all that is different
or strange to us.

In doing so,
they do a disservice to us all,
all we ordinary folk
who revel in the understanding:
that all are equal
under the protections
provided by this nation's founders
and those that followed;
that fear is the enemy of hope;
that directed hatred
is the path to a divided
and broken nation;
and that the rejection of change

Rhetoric

is a rejection of adaptation
to the influx of new ideas
and vision
that has helped bring greatness
to this nation
of immigrants,
of migrants,
and refugees.

It seems to me
that we should be careful
in what we say
and what we do
as much in times of perceived crisis
as in the tranquil times.

It is easy to be mindful
of our neighbor's rights
when we see no threat
to us and ours.

It is just as easy to forget
in times of turmoil and discontent
that our neighbor's rights
are in fact our own
and that reducing theirs
ultimately diminishes the rights of all.

For after all,
our neighbors and we
are not so very different.

At the end of the day,
we all want the same basic things;
food,
water,
clothing,

family,
and shelter –
a place to call home
if only in the moments of our use.

We are united
in our common understanding
that liberty is not a gift.
It is an inalienable right
that should not be restricted
or abridged
in the name of personal
or national security.

So it is
that we must stand and be counted,
make our voices heard against the din
or else in silence
bear the weight
of decisions made in our stead,
by those who know no better
but who have shouted louder
and longer
than those who do.

In the confusion
of whispered lies
and shouted "truths",
of action sought
and decisions made,
we may find that we have lost
that which makes us
as we are
with rights and liberties
abjured and forgot
in the frenzied hunt for enemies
across the street,

Rhetoric

down the block,
and even in our very homes.

And in the dawning light
of the new day
find that the enemy
for whom we search
has become ourselves.

Immigrants

They were simple folk,
and uneducated
at least in the way
most would think of it.

They had no skills to offer,
no technical
or professional degrees.

They were poor,
hungry,
and sometimes downtrodden
with barely the clothes
upon their backs
to call their own.

But they had dreams,
dreams of a better life
far away from their past,
far away from violence,
poverty,
injustice,
and war.

All they wanted was a chance,
a chance to work hard,
to earn a living,
to lift themselves
and their families
to a better way of life,
to a future bright with promise
and with hope.

And so they came,

Rhetoric

eyes downcast at the prospect
of being denied entry,
of having their dreams dashed
by those who no longer dream
the dream of their grandparents,
by those who do not appreciate
how far their families have come,
by those who have forgotten
that those who came before them
were simple folk
pursuing freedom,
pursuing work,
pursuing opportunity
by leaving home,
facing danger,
enduring hardship,
and the loss of everything
they had and knew
for the chance of a better life
for themselves
and their children
by becoming
immigrants.

Religious Liberty

"I disagree with your beliefs."

"That's fine. I respect that. I'd like to have a plain cake donut please."

"I can't sell you one."

"What? … Why can't you sell me a donut?"

"The Supreme Court says that I, as the owner of a shop, do not have to sell to anyone that my religious beliefs find objectionable."

"I'm not sure that the Supreme Court actually meant it that way but Ok… what about my beliefs do you find objectionable?"

"Do you cross yourself left to right or right to left?"

"Ummm… Actually, I don't cross myself."

"Oh… you one of them Muslims then?"

"No. No I'm not."

"A Jew?"

"No."

"One of them Hindus or Sikhs then?"

"Nope. Not either of them… although I find some of their beliefs fascinating."

Rhetoric

"Then you must be a Buddhist... always getting on about Nirvana and such."

"Sorry. I respect Buddhists for their beliefs, but I do not share them."

"Shinto?"

"Nope."

"Confucian?"

"No."

"Catholic... Mormon... Methodist?"

"No, No, and No."

"Well surely you're not one of them Anglican folks?"

"No, I am not."

"Well what are you then? ... Wait... you're gay aren't you? Or maybe transgender..."

"Not that it's any of your business but no and no again but I do find it offensive that you would somehow imply that they don't have religious beliefs."

"Ok then. Why don't you tell me what you believe in."

"Well actually I'm an atheist. I respect all the religions you've mentioned but I don't follow the tenets of any of them. There are some very good teachings in all of them, but I don't think that any really capture the reality of existence."

"So you don't believe in God?"

"No. But I do believe in human rights… that all folks are equal and should be treated as such… that no one religion or philosophy has a monopoly on the understanding of this existence or what's in the human heart… that no one has the right to tell others who they can and can't love, what choices they should make, or how they should live their lives as long as they respect the rights of others to do the same."

"Ah. I see."

"So how about that plain cake donut?"

"I can't sell it to you. I disagree with your beliefs."

Rhetoric

Truth

Truth is elusive.
Is it perception or fact?
Is it what we believe
or what exists?
Are there shades of gray
or simply black or white?

Where does the sun go
when it is night?
Why does thunder come
in the midst of storm?
How did the Earth form
at the beginning of time?

The bird is dead.
Fact.
What killed it?
Arrogance?
Hunger?
Fashion?
Jobs?
Or a shotgun?
Is intent important
if the end result is the same?

The Passenger Pigeon is gone.
Does it matter how it vanished
or is it something
simply to be accepted
as the new way of things?

The ice shelf disappears.
Does it matter why?
Is it important

to address the facts
or simply accept
that change is inevitable,
that regardless of intent
actions have consequences
beyond what was foreseen
when those actions were taken?

Earthquakes happen every day.
Does it matter
that none occurred before?
Should we be concerned
that something is different now?
Should we seek to know why?
Should we try to find the causes
and by knowing end them
or simply close our eyes
and ride the shocks to sleep?

The mine has closed.
Did the jobs go overseas?
Did it cost too much to operate
under safe conditions,
with a fair wage?
Were other technologies
just better,
cleaner,
more economical to use?

Either way,
folks are out of work
and hope becomes a desperate thing
when hunger's at the door,
bills cannot be paid,
and tomorrow is no certain thing.

The birds are dead.

Rhetoric

The ice shelf is gone.
Earthquakes are present every day.
The mine is closed.

Facts.
Our understanding of why
and whether it is important to care
depends as much upon our beliefs,
and our self-interested interpretation,
as upon cold data and statistics
showing the way things are.

Is a lie a lie
if it is believed to be the truth?
Is a fact untrue
if it conflicts with one's beliefs
or is in opposition to
a desired course of action?

Should we try to resurrect the past
and return things to what they were?
Should we understand why things are
and try to prevent an unkind future?
Should we simply accept the changes
as the natural course of things
with no thought to stem
the flow of events yet to come?
Should we simply ignore what is
as though events had never happened
in hopes that the world will right itself
without some intervention?

The birds are still dead.
The ice is still gone.
The earthquakes still occur.
The mine is still closed.

Perhaps it is better
that the passenger pigeons have disappeared,
that the ice is vanishing,
that earthquakes happen more frequently,
that the mine is closed.

But perhaps it is not.
Perhaps each piece of the story
tells of greater changes yet ahead,
of more vanishings,
of a hotter world,
of instability beneath our feet
as the world changes,
and technology ends some things
and makes others possible.

The birds will not come back
though others may yet be saved.

The ice may yet be restored
if it be deemed necessary
for our survival.

New earthquakes may be prevented
if we understand the causes
and act to change conditions.

Old jobs may be restored
but should they be
in all cases,
in all places,
as technology opens new opportunities,
new jobs,
new futures
for those able
to take advantage of the change?

Rhetoric

Truth versus belief.
Fact versus perception.
Understanding versus self-interest.
Sometimes they match
and folks work together
to achieve a greater good.

More often they do not
and decision to act,
or not,
is marred by conflicting,
opposing goals
driven by belief,
informed by perception,
and powered by self-interest
despite the facts,
despite an understanding
of how things are
and how they may yet be
as the future closes fast upon us.

Truth is elusive.
Whether we find it,
unvarnished,
in all its cold hard reality
or see it through the filter
of our perceptions,
hopes,
and desires,
will determine what future,
if any,
yet awaits.

Guns

"Guns don't kill people.
People kill people."

A stupid thing to think
at a time like this,
but I couldn't help it,
it just popped into my head
when the gunshots started
and people all around
started falling to the ground
some alive,
some not,
and the world narrowed down
to a choice
of who to help,
where to run,
where to hide
as bullets smacked
against the ground
and objects
and folks
nearby.

"People kill people."
kept repeating in my head
But it's a hell of a lot easier
with whatever gun
whoever is shooting at us
is using up there,
somewhere out of sight,
and beyond my ability to reach.

Maybe whoever it is
has been beyond reach

Rhetoric

for a long time now
but that's no comfort
as the shots ring out,
the bullets fall like leaden rain,
and I wait,
wondering if I'll be next,
if I'll ever see home again,
if they'll mention me
on the nightly news,
and my friends and family
will find out I'm gone.

"Guns don't kill people.
People kill people."

A brave face

He was rich.
He was famous.
He was powerful in the industry.
He was a strong religious man.
He was beloved in the community.

She was young.
She was vulnerable.
She was in no position to say
"No."
She was beholden to him
for her success,
for her job,
for her wellbeing,
for her sense of self.

So when he told her
what he wanted,
she did not think
she could refuse,
did not believe
that she had any choice
but to go along
and do as he asked,
do as he demanded
regardless of the cost
she would bear
forever.

After all,
wasn't this the price she had to pay
to become what she wanted,
to go where she wished,
to get her dream job,

Rhetoric

to escape the hell
of a broken family,
of a life of poverty,
to be part of the game?

If she said "No",
she would lose this chance,
lose this opportunity
to be more than what she was,
to make her dreams come true
and this break
might never come again.

So she didn't say "No",
didn't say anything at all
as she let him do what he wanted,
enduring it until he was done,
and then smiled through clenched teeth
as he thanked her for her time,
told her he would call
when the decision was made,
the part assigned,
the job given.

And as she left,
gathering herself together,
she told herself
that it didn't matter,
that it was just a small thing,
a necessary thing
and that her feelings
of shame and anger
at herself and him
would fade over time
'til she could forget
and put it all behind.

But even with that thought,
she knew it wasn't true,
knew she could never forget,
knew that what had happened
would color all that followed
regardless if she got the job,
regardless of where she went from here,
regardless of any success
she might achieve.

Whether the experience
would harden or destroy her
only time would tell.
But she would never talk of this,
never let anyone know
of her anger and her shame,
never tell
how she had let him have his way
because she'd felt
she'd had no choice,
no good way out
of the situation.

And as she turned away,
merging with the passing crowd,
putting on a brave face
for the outside world,
inside, she cried.

Rhetoric

In for a penny

When does absolutism
overcome common sense?

Should political expediency
ever outweigh due process?

Why do present folk
often pay the price
for punishments deferred
or denied in the past?

At what point
does a crowd seeking justice
become a torch bearing mob?

Stealing a penny
is not the same
as stealing a million dollars
but absolutism treats it so
demanding the maximum penalty
for any infraction
with punishment
often coming before judgement.

With process lost,
with judgement forgot,
who then is immune
when fingers are pointed,
the accusations start,
and the crowd descends
lighting torches as they go?

When the righteous stand up
and sins are revealed

with great gnashing of teeth
and wailing that any,
any should be imperfect,
regardless of the nature of their defect,
then all are lost.

All are subject to accusation
while the most grievous offenders
hide in plain sight,
often in the front ranks of the accusers,
as examples are made,
past failures are redressed,
and the fires fueled
by past silence and inaction
are quenched by the offering
of sacrificial victims
who, regardless of their faults,
may not deserve the punishment
embraced by those seeking absolution.

Once fires are quenched
and reason rises once again
those left standing are often
the ones who admit no wrong,
who sneer at the thought of imperfection,
who ignore the cries for punishment,
who use absolutism
as a weapon against those
who would stand against them
while good folk,
who acknowledge fault,
are cast aside.

All have failed in some measure.
All are imperfect in some way.
All should quail before the thought
of having their entire life

Rhetoric

searched for inequity,
and once found,
having sins and faults
held up for all to see.

But all sins are not the same.
All crimes are not equal
in their nature,
in their horror
and their shame,
and punishments
should be measured
and suited to the fault so seen.

For stealing a penny
is not the same
as stealing a million dollars
though some would make it so.

Heroes

We live in an age of heroes
although they would not think it so.

They are no different
from you or me.
They love,
hate,
are selfish,
and selfless,
and rejoice in the little things
and the large,
and sorrow
when loss intrudes upon life.

They put their shoes on,
or their boots,
like the rest of us.
They make plans
and talk about the future
like we all do from time to time.

They get up every day
and leave to do their jobs.
They kiss their spouses
and their children goodbye.
They laugh.
They cry.
They live each day
and, in the fullness of time,
will die.

They are no different.
But when they leave
to do their tasks,

Rhetoric

they know
that they may not come back,
that in the act of doing their job,
they might be called upon
to sacrifice all
in doing their duty,
protecting their country,
preserving their honor
and that of all who serve
or look to them to guard
against the troubles in the night
or the fires of the day
that might otherwise consume all.

The choices are hard.
The chances of failure many.
But still they go into the morning sun
or the dark of night
to do what must be done,
to do what others will not,
to do their jobs
in the face of challenge,
in the face of adversity,
in the face of horror,
with the ever-present chance
that accident or fate
will grant them no reprieve,
will give them no return
to those they love
and the life they left behind.

But they give no thought of that,
these ordinary folk
going about their work.
Yet they are heroes
in all the many ways
one would measure

such a thing
as they go where we would not,
do what we would not,
give what we would not.

And if they should give their all,
if they should not return,
we must honor
these ordinary folk,
our brothers,
sisters,
fathers,
and mothers
for all that they have done
to keep us safe,
to give us the better world
that they will never see.

Although they would not think it so,
we live in an age of heroes.

Rhetoric

When the caisson rolls

When the caisson rolls,
the rifles fire,
the bugle sounds,
and the flag is handed down,
who takes the measure
of the one within?

Who accuses them
of somehow being less,
of being different,
of being unworthy
of the honors being given,
the rifle salute,
the sounding horn,
and the folded cloth?

Can anyone,
in the moment
when the family
and friends
and onlookers
cast their flowers
and the dirt,
say it matters
how the one they mourn
viewed themselves,
what they believed,
or how they lived their life
beyond the claim of duty,
beyond the call to service,
beyond their dedication
to the common good
that led them here
to this place,

this moment,
this end,
when the caisson rolls?

Rhetoric

We are all one

One.

We are all one underneath it all.
Hearts pumping.
Blood flowing freely through our veins.
We are all daughters and sons,
children of a god
that does not recognize
anything but the color
of our souls,
with the shades made manifest
by our desires,
our thoughts,
our words,
and our deeds.

There is no different flesh
despite our perceptions,
despite the fear felt
at the sight of someone
different in the smallest of things,
hair,
eyes,
speech,
hue,
faith,
gender,
all meaningless
in the bigger picture.

It is after all
a learned thing,
to fear the difference,
acquired

through endless repetitions
and lessons from those
that miss the point,
who do not recognize themselves
in others,
who do not practice
what they preach,
who are content
to be separate
in a way that engenders strife
instead of peace,
that builds on fears
instead of the hopes
that all share
underneath the surface things
that mark us as distinct
from each other.

Remember,
the next time,
that to them
you are the other
the one who is different,
the one to be feared,
or hated,
or ignored,
or pushed aside,
because that is what
they were taught
by circumstance,
and by those
whose interests were served
to make it so.

Then perhaps,
just perhaps,
you will look

Rhetoric

to see the sameness
there before you,
to see them
as you in another form,
as a fellow traveler
between the sign posts on the way,
as another life
as worthy as yours
with all its possibilities
and potential.

For we are all one underneath it all.

Accidental Extinction

It was an accident really,
a vagary of chance.
We built a road,
felled the trees,
burned the fields,
planted a crop,
drilled for oil,
then for gas,
and they died by the hundreds.

How were we supposed to know
there were only hundreds of their kind,
isolated,
alone
in that particular piece of woods,
in that particular forest,
on that particular parcel of land?

Hell.
We didn't even know they existed
'til we found one.
Just one
in the last stretch to be developed,
in the last untouched piece of nature
to be found for miles around.

We saved it.
Put it on display in the local town
but we haven't found any more
'cept for the remains of all the others.
Oh, we recognize them now
'cause we know what to look for
since we found that one.

Rhetoric

I'd like to think
that it would've been different
had we known ahead of time,
that we could've saved them all somehow.
But it wouldn't 've made no difference
in the end.

Expanding fields,
an oil spill,
shoot,
the sheer garbage of daily life
would've done them in
'til we still would've had
just that last one,
an oddity in its singularness
down there in that town.

It still would've been an accident.
We wouldn't 've meant them no harm.
But at least we could've
watched their numbers dwindle.
Could've convinced ourselves
that we did our best,
really we did,
to help them survive.

But this way ...
Hell.
We didn't even know they were there.

Those who do not learn from history

The professor leaned forward
warming to his topic.
His companion listened
as he talked.

"A demagogue
with no experience in politics
playing to the basest instincts
of the people.
Selling fear.
Playing on the anxiety
of the underclass
of the unemployed,
the underemployed,
the uneducated,
and the poor.

A savior to lead them
to the promised land
where the nation
would be great again,
with all enemies defeated
and the complicit and corrupt
politicians and powerbrokers
brought down
and put in their places

With the use of scapegoats
to reassure the people
that it is not their fault
that everything will be all right
if only we eliminate them
and return society
to how it should be,

Rhetoric

how it was
when all was right with the world.

Once in power
putting folk of similar beliefs
in positions of authority
would give control
over the intelligence
and security apparatus
to be used ruthlessly
to suppress opposition
and blackmail any
who would stand against him.

Action against the media;
Strict press laws
to make owners and journalists
libel for accurate reporting
and views opposing government moves

Acquisition of media outlets
by those in sympathy
with the leader's goals,
Intimidation of the rest
through arrests,
seizures,
audits,
and law suits,
would neuter and replace
a free press
with one more compliant
and supportive of the leader.

A concerted campaign
designed to stoke fear
of enemies abroad and within
would provide cover

for restrictions on civil liberties,
voting rights,
and even opposing political activity.
Only cronies,
crooks,
and opportunists
would profit in an economic system
shackled and restrained.

And once complete control is assured
with foreign wars
and internal repression
the means of ensuring compliance,
all would be lost,
ideology imposed,
liberty eschewed,
and democracy would vanish
like a dream upon waking
in the cold light of dawn."

His companion replied,
"Surely Professor,
you are speaking
of today's political environment,
with all the insults and hate baiting,
the innuendo and fear mongering,
the scapegoating,
and the drive to invoke our lesser selves
in the name of jobs,
in the name of security,
in the name of national greatness.
Surely this is all a reference
to what could occur
if a certain candidate succeeds."

Rhetoric

The professor paused,
hand halted in mid gesture,
eyes open wide in surprise and shock.
"Oh God no!
I have no interest in that.
I'm a historian.
I was describing Hitler
and the end of the Weimar Republic.
Who did you think
I was talking about?"

Grieco

Think three times
(For Liu Xiaobo)

Think three times before speaking
and then think again.

Be circumspect.
Be cautious.
Do not speak your mind.

Do not speak
of truths
or rights
or all that may be wrong.

For if you do
you may be arrested.
You may be jailed.
You may find yourself alone
with none to talk to
or listen
for the rest of your days
until you find yourself,
at the last,
too sick
to wonder at the justice of it,
too weak to rage
against the dimming of vision,
the dying of the light,
and the regime
that makes it so.

But if you do not speak,
no one will.
If you do not fight
for justice,

Rhetoric

for the rights of all
and one,
if you do not raise your voice
amidst the silence,
then who will speak the truth,
who will right the wrongs
all see
but will not talk of,
who will be the one
for those who follow
to whisper of
as they find the courage,
first to think
and then to act,
to end what should not be?

Think three times before speaking
but then speak.

Be forthright.
Be outspoken.
Be courageous,
in the face
of what is yet to come,
and change the world.

Grieco

Blood and treasure

You cannot save a country
if you are the enemy,
if you represent the evils
that the people come to see
as a danger to their culture,
within which they all thrive,
for which they'll fight forever
though it cost their very lives.

They shook our hands in daylight
and shot at us at night.
They used their skills against us
when we taught them how to fight.
They were not our enemies
but we were surely theirs
from the farm fields to the markets
where we helped them sell their wares.

We did not understand them.
They knew us all too well.
We could not tell just who they were
in the places where they dwelled.
Our friends resembled enemies
and enemies our friends
and when we knew the difference
it was far too late by then.

They fought us in the cities.
They fought us in the fields
and though we killed vast numbers
the rest would never yield.
They merged into the background
where they waited for their time
while we dreamed of victory

Rhetoric

amidst the dirt and grime.

We could not leave the battle
for then they'd surely win.
We would take the long road
though our chances there were thin.
We'd spend our blood and treasure,
attrition it would be,
'til one of us gave up the fight,
withdrawn for all to see.

We'd say that we'd won the war
while they'd know we did not
and so we'd leave a land we hoped
that history had forgot.
But history will remember,
as scholars seek to find,
the truths we sought to bury
in the land we left behind.

And once we'd left their country,
they'd finish all the strife
by use of cherished ballot box
or by the bloody knife.
And nothing we'd have done there,
could stop that final fight
as they settled all their ancient scores
and set the world aright.

And in the years to follow,
we'd justify the war
for we had so much invested
in blood and treasure stored
beneath the fertile valleys,
beneath the desert sands,
we surely didn't fight in vain
to save that foreign land

from the desperate enemy,
from the fearsome foe,
who fought to save their country
from the ones who laid it low.
For they were only patriots,
those faithful, favored few,
who fought for God and country
'gainst the foreign threat they knew.

You cannot save a country
if you are the enemy,
if you represent the evils
that the people come to see
as a danger to their culture,
within which they all thrive,
for which they'll fight forever
though it cost their very lives.

Rhetoric

One Word

My mind is not what it once was.
It is more and less than that,
a puzzle of light and shadow,
a maze of forgotten necessities
and remembered niceties.

I had forgotten a word,
but what a word.
It spanned the difference
between them and us,
between stranger
and welcomed friend,
between foreigner
and belovéd countryman.

One word to do all that.
It identifies us.
It marks us as distinct,
unlike the others
who have no claim to it.

Say it,
and everyone understands.
It implies shared ideals,
a commonness of purpose,
and a way of life
envied and hated
because it exists,
a contrast to the way others live.
A burden and a gift,
this one word creates expectations
for what we are
and are not,
for how we should behave,

for what we should do
as individuals,
as groups,
and as a united whole.

This one word makes us family
where none existed
and bears the gift of freedom
in the face of adversity
to those too long denied it.

It is a call to battle
and a call to peace.
It is a cause and a reason,
a question and an explanation.

It unites and divides
but spans the gulf between
haves and have nots,
granting to all the right to dream,
to hope for better lives
and providing the means
to make it so.

I had forgotten,
forgotten
that one word held such power,
that one word could,
alone and unadorned,
have so much meaning,
could shape and define
a person,
a people,
a country,
and a way of life.

I had forgotten

Rhetoric

but I remember now
for it marks all we were,
what we are,
and what we shall yet become.

I had forgotten
but I remember now
the millions whose toil,
whose sacrifice,
whose lives
made mine possible.

I had forgotten
but I remember now
the word I carry with pride
emblazoned in my very being,
the word that marks us
as individuals,
as a people,
and as a nation,
as distinct and special
unlike any others
before or since,
blessed with one vision,
united in diversity,
and sworn
to the preservation of liberty.

One word,
American.

I had forgotten
but I remember now.

The coming season

Enjoy the coming season.
It may be the last we have.

No one can see the future
except as glimmers
past the window of today.
It shifts.
It changes by the deeds done now.

We plan
but we cannot assure
that fortune
will smile on our endeavors.

We save
but we cannot say for what.

The future is as it will be.
It is beyond our grasp
and shall not be
as we envision it now.

The plate is broken.
If it is mended
can it be what it was before?

The wheel has turned.
Can we have it retrace its route
and stop
to improve the course taken?

They say
we are the sum of all we were.
I say

Rhetoric

it is what we are that makes us us
and being creatures of choice
we can choose to be what we wish.

We can remake ourselves
in our own image
without the boundaries
and restraints
some might think would pattern us.

There is no fixed plan.
(There is
but we are not shaped by it.)
We are constrained
only by ourselves
and need not fear,
or hate,
or love
except by choice,
except by need
to rationalize our decisions.

Civilizations rise.
Civilizations fall.
It is all the same.

Religions bind.
Reason loosens the ties
but keeps the ones
most comfortable to us.

Belief is a drug.
Reason the cure
that cuts through illusions
and false justifications.

Beware the one

who knows all things,
who is omnipotent,
who casts the world
as white and black,
right and wrong,
good and evil.
That one
will take your choice from you.
That one
will have you comfortably bound
with reason left on holiday.

With belief,
one does not need to think.

Without thought
there is no reason.

Without reason,
there is no choice.

Without choice,
all futures are the same
with tomorrow
a cold and barren place.

Enjoy the coming season.
It may be the last we have.

Rhetoric

The Heavens Wept

The heavens wept
at the sight of ordinary men
in extraordinary times
leaving their homes
and lives behind
to serve the common good,
mortgaging their futures,
their hopes and dreams,
so that their families,
their sons and daughters,
parents and wives,
could live secure
and safe from harm
far from the pain
and anguish
that accompanies the thousand ways
a man can die
even if he survives
the immediate battle,
the urgency of the moment,
the despair
that comes with imminent defeat
and the joy
amidst the bone numbing tiredness
when he is still after all alive
when all around
have fallen into still repose
from which they shall not rise again.

They fall by the thousands
and the tens of thousands
but for each who falls
there comes another to carry on,
to persevere in the face of horror,

Grieco

in the face of loss
profound and deep
as brothers bound by hardship,
joined by adversity,
lose their kin
in quick ways
and in slow
throughout the gathering twilight,
throughout the lingering days
of choking dust
and sucking mud,
of endless sun
and unceasing rain,
of noisome life
and quiet death.

In the end,
the carnage
claims more than any can know.
Hopes crushed,
dreams dashed
upon the field of battle,
souls battered
by visions of a world
twisted by the need to survive,
the imperative to persevere,
to achieve victory
in the name of a greater good,
without which all is lost,
without which
there is no dream to return to,
without which
the agony of war,
borne by the watchful dead
and the present living,
would not be worth the cost in time,
would not be worth the cost in resources,

Rhetoric

would not be worth the cost in blood
split upon the waiting earth,
spent to purchase fleeting things,
a way of life,
a culture unbowed and unbending,
with things the way they were before,
before the price was known,
before the world was changed
by the act of saving it,
all sides
acting according to their righteous claims,
all done with the thought
that tomorrow will be better than today,
that their cause is just,
and that the enemy
must be stopped at any cost
to keep it so.

Some would say
the price is too high
and they would be correct.
The loss of one
is more cost than any
should be willing to bear,
the loss of ten
a burden to the soul,
the loss of thousands
an ever-present hemorrhage,
the loss of millions
unspeakable
in its impact on the future
present when combat is done,
the issue settled,
the cost tallied,
and the price paid.

Grieco

And if there are victors,
they will praise their God
for their victory
and write the history
so that the future
will remember their past,
their reasons,
and the right of it,
to justify why it was needful,
to justify the loss
of those ordinary men
in extraordinary times
as the earth waited,
the dead watched,
and the heavens wept.

Rhetoric

What value?

What is the value of a human life?
Ten dollars?
A thousand?
A Million?

What if it were your daughter,
your son,
your wife or husband,
your mom or dad
that lay there
helpless
with doctors
and medical knowledge
and technology
as their only hope
for survival?

Would any amount of money
be too little
or too much
if a dollar more,
or a thousand,
or a million
would make them whole,
restore them to health,
or least to a semblance
of what they were before?

Where do we set the mark
between survival and death,
between hope and despair,
between economic value
and human life?

Society can help pay the cost
or leave it to the individual.
It can provide the best care
or only what is affordable.
It can provide for all
or leave folk to their own device,
to only what they can afford,
to only what is measurable
by dollars and cents
and by doing so
set the value of a human life.

Rhetoric

Imprisoned though my spirit be

Imprisoned though my spirit be,
I am, within, myself.

You told me to stop singing
so I stopped.

You told me not to dance
so I did not.

You told me not to talk so loud
so I whispered.

You told me not to run
so I walked.

You told me not to drink
and so I sipped acceptable things.

You told me not to do this
and that
and all the things I loved
and I complied
for to do otherwise
was unthinkable
in a world
where your words are law
and laws
mean only what you say they do.

You told me what to think
but that you cannot force
although you limit
what I hear and see
and restrict my access

to a greater world.

You tell me what to believe
but I refuse to believe
that anyone can make that so.

You tell me how to worship
but only God can rule me
in that regard
and you are not God.

So it is that I await,
like a bird,
within my soul
to be set free.

Rhetoric

Your Right to Vote
(A Cautionary Tale)

Your Right to vote is sacred
enshrined in the constitution
and protected by the laws of this land.

Your Right to vote is sacred
but if you cannot pass
a few simple tests
you are not fit
to exercise that right.

Your Right to vote is sacred
but restrictions to prevent fraud
can ensure that certain folk
may be excluded.

Your Right to vote is sacred
but if we control
who lives within the district
we can ensure that the votes of our folk
will count for more.

Your Right to vote is sacred
but if we shorten the voting hours
not everyone will be able to
with those closest gaining an advantage
and those farthest away
being inconvenienced.

Your Right to vote is sacred
but if we reduce the voting locations
and put them where our folk live
some undesirables will not come
or will just give up

due to distance and transport
and time and bother
and our folks' votes will be magnified
by the absence.

Your Right to vote is sacred
but if we change the law and rules
just so
we can control whether and where
and when and if you vote.

And if we can do that
we can control the election
and who may be elected.

And if we can do that
we can control the States
and the Country.

And if we can do that
we can decide what laws are written
and what the Constitution means
and what your rights are.

Your right to vote is sacred.

Rhetoric

Fever dream

If it can be done to one,
it can be done to all.
The first right denied,
the first wrongful imprisonment,
leads to more
until no one is safe.

It happens slowly at first,
almost unnoticed
in the tumult of the day,
buried beneath the hue and cry
of the current crisis
and the attempt
to secure the rights of one group
while denying rights to others.

But soon,
all too soon,
the pace quickens
until,
in a blur of motion,
the right to obey
becomes the only right that remains
with all else but an afterthought
as folk surrender to their fear
and embrace security
as a reasonable substitute for freedom,
embrace jobs
as a replacement for rights,
embrace the rule of one,
or just a select few,
to replace the will
and common sense

of the many.

Once that occurs,
it is difficult to stop
as pace quickens
and right after right
become but afterthoughts
disappearing
as though they'd never been real,
were never held as sacred,
had never existed
except as fevered dreams
of the dispossessed,
the downtrodden,
and the powerless.

Once given up,
once taken,
they cannot be restored,
they cannot be reclaimed
without abundant civil strife
that wipes away complacency
and awakens the common folk
to their loss,
that quickens the pulse of liberty
within their veins,
and halts the spreading stain of tyrrany.

Even then,
it may not be enough
with imprisonment
and the rule of law
employed to quash rebellion
and dissent,
until voices are silenced,
fear replaces hope

Rhetoric

and the good and rights
of the many
become subordinate
to the will and desires
of the few.

If it can be done to one,
it can be done to all.

Grieco

Rhetoric

Grieco

People look away
because they do not want to see.

If they saw,
they would have to think.

If they thought,
they would have to decide.

If they decided,
they would have to act.

If they acted,
they would be bound by those actions
and be responsible for them,
each and every one.

People look away
because they do not want to see.

Grieco

ABOUT THE AUTHOR

Born and raised in a small rural town, the author left to pursue higher education and a career which took him to different parts of the world. After a lifetime listening to the whisper of the wind, the burble of a brook, and the sound of songbirds all imparting their wisdom, he's returned to his roots, spending his days as a country gentleman, taking the time now and then to put some words on paper.